T0001188

" *Humans smile with so little provocation.* "

MR. SPOCK'S
LITTLE BOOK OF
MINDFULNESS

STAR TREK™

This book is a light-hearted exploration of the wisdom of Mr. Spock from the STAR TREK TV show and is not intended as a serious guide to mindfulness. Unless you are half-Vulcan already, it will not enable you to overcome your emotional side, any more than it will teach you how to perform the Vulcan nerve pinch or mind-meld with a rock creature. As a look at human life from an alien point of view it may serve as a mildly helpful and occasionally amusing perspective. To expect to achieve true enlightenment from a book of TV quotes and cartoons is not logical.

Published by **Hero Collector Books**, a division of Eaglemoss Ltd. 2020
1st Floor, Beaumont House, Kensington Village, Avonmore Road,
W14 8TS, London, UK.

™ & © 2020 CBS Studios Inc. © 2020 Paramount Pictures Corp.
STAR TREK and related marks and logos are trademarks of CBS Studios Inc.
All Rights Reserved.

All rights reserved. No part of this publication may be reproduced, stored in a retrieval system or transmitted in any form or by any means, electronic, mechanical, photocopying, recording or otherwise, without the prior permission of the publisher.

Artist and writer: Glenn Dakin
Designer: Katy Everett
General Editor: Ben Robinson
Project Manager: Jo Bourne
Sub-editor: Alice Peebles

www.herocollector.com

ISBN 978-1-85875-953-1

10 9 8 7 6 5 4 3 2 1

Printed in China

CONTENTS

INTRODUCTION

> " *Live long and prosper.* "

The well-known Vulcan saying captures the essence of this curious race. The simple phrase reveals kindness under a formal cloak. But how does a Vulcan live long and prosper? It is done by living a life we might describe as mindful.

Vulcans do not seek shallow pleasures. They would rather study ancient Vulcan poetry than look at funny pictures of cats online. *They don't seek riches,* preferring the **WEALTH OF KNOWLEDGE**.

Even the pursuit of happiness is not on their agenda, A Vulcan seeks fulfillment, not fun. Of course, there is the occasional small pleasure of winning an argument over an annoying colleague *(Are you listening, Dr. McCoy?)*, or possibly saving the universe from total annihilation, but a Vulcan would be slow to admit even these satisfactions. *They know how to keep it inside*.

Vulcans almost destroyed their home world many centuries ago in a series of wars, and so abandoned all emotion. They gave up the urge to follow their desires and replaced it with a **COOL, LOGICAL OUTLOOK**.

To some, the cold Vulcan is all they see. But there is more to these dignified people: they are protectors of diversity and truth. They are open-minded beings who can converse with whales, side with rock monsters, and come back from the dead *(occasionally)*.

In the pursuit of a fulfilling life, logic is their tool. *They use it to search for truth*. With it, they find a way to accept life as it is. This quality speaks clearly to us humans at a time when we find our own world seems to have turned into a slightly mad parallel universe.

And in our search for sanity, we have begun to conjure with the word mindfulness – and find it... **FASCINATING**.

1

ON FOCUS

Are you able to concentrate on one thing at a time? Ever since some bright spark at IBM computers invented the word "multitasking" in the sixties **(AND IT WAS FOR MACHINES)** we have become almost ashamed of doing one thing at time. Not any more. Free yourself from the need to learn Ferengi while driving the kids to school – *Vulcan mindfulness can lead you to the beautiful simplicity of... unitasking.*

Mr. Spock knows the clarity of focused thinking. When a planet-killing Doomsday machine is about to swallow your starship, it's important not to start checking your mail or stopping to share a cool picture of your impending destruction on WhatsApp. This might sound obvious, but we humans are very similarly distracted when in our own daily *"doomsday scenarios,"* like messaging the boss or changing lanes on the highway while updating our playlist.

Social media is probably our worst downfall. An unending source of distraction, it gets in the way of

" Curious how often you humans manage to obtain that which you do not want. ,,

focus — the very thing we need to get stuff done. Also, more worryingly, it has given us humans the pressure to share and be interesting. This would not be a problem for Spock. A Vulcan is far more concerned with being interested than interesting.

Private as a race, Vulcans would not post much on Spacebook **(or whatever they have in the 23rd century)**. It would not be logical for a Vulcan to reveal his holiday location to virtual strangers. Nor would it seem a practical use of his time to Photoshop a kitten wearing a tie and possibly add the word **ME-WOW** to the image. A Vulcan will take a selfie only if he wants to check on the progress of a blackhead and there is no mirror available.

A Vulcan is not big on *"sharing."* None of Spock's human colleagues even know his real name – which he claims it would take them several days to learn how to pronounce. Up until his *Enterprise* mission, he had never even told his human mother that he loved her. No doubt he often found time to ask her where the eyebrow tweezers were. Eyebrows that good take focus.

Vulcans are taught from an early age to concentrate on a single task until it is completed. Not for them knitting a woolly cover for their communicator in front of the television. If it was Mr. Spock's intention to watch TV all night, he would do so with full attention. He would understand the whole plot and know all the characters' names. He would not, after a third glass

of Saurian brandy, be wondering why that blonde
– *whose name he can't remember* – tried to
kill her husband, or was it her brother, or are they all
alien replicas? He would certainly not have messaged
OMG!!! to humankind in general when the big season
finale reveal took place.

We are increasingly vulnerable to media that invests
billions of dollars in the art of grabbing our attention.
That money would be wasted on a Vulcan.

"I've never stopped to look at clouds before, or rainbows," Spock admits.

Such a person is unlikely to begin checking out pictures of cute tribbles before he searches for that data he needs to save the ship from an alien god. That's why Spock has the facts at his fingertips and few invitations to join fan groups for hairless pets.

Learning from Vulcan focus, we can strive to shut out the attractions and distractions that seduce **OUR EVERY WAKING HOUR**. And if we get our work done with Vulcan efficiency — well, it leaves time to look at kitten memes afterward anyway.

> **"** *Computers make excellent and efficient servants, but I have no wish to serve under them.* **"**

S pock has often been likened to a computer, so it is ironic that he is so little in awe of them. Taking a leaf from his book can help us to de-stress about machines. They bug us so much, because we depend on them so much. SO, DEPEND LESS.

With computer-like brains, Vulcans have less need of technology, preferring to develop their own minds. To a Vulcan, quietly exploring the mind is an endless source of diversion. There are mathematical paradoxes to solve, 348-verse Vulcan lullabies to memorize, 3-D chess stratagems to muse over. The next time you are tempted to reach for your gadget for entertainment, why not try reaching into your mind for it instead? There are memories in there – or perhaps fantasies (YOU KNOW THE ONE) that can be far more exciting than a Twitter update. A developed mind goes with you everywhere, doesn't run low on battery, and doesn't start bleeping in the cinema.

A trained mind gives a Vulcan experiences unknown to us. For example, if they need a rest, instead of going on an expensive vacation, a Vulcan can simply go into a trance, switching bodily functions to standby. Admittedly, this is unlikely to generate cool Instagram images of Borg beach parties to make your friends jealous. But on the upside, you are far less likely to lose your luggage, catch Rigellian tree fever, or be found by your ex lying outside an Orion nightclub sobbing, "Nobody loves me."

2

ON KEEPING
AN OPEN MIND

Ever been threatened by a glowing green hand the size of a football stadium? Or swallowed by a cosmic ameba? Perhaps you've had your brain stolen? Mr. Spock has faced all these seemingly impossible things. He knows the value of keeping an open mind – because in his line of work, literally anything can happen.

An open mind is a vital asset in exploration, so it is logical for Mr. Spock to keep one. That eerie glow that just appeared in front of your starship could be about to destroy you, or it could be a portal to another universe. Or it could be a living being in itself. Frankly, it very often is the latter – **AND WITH AN AMERICAN ACCENT, TOO**.

One of the most treasured Spock phrases of all is: *"It's life, Jim, but not as we know it."* Like many great screen quotes, he never actually said this precisely, but you get the idea. Life but not as we know it has included a creature made of rock, a salt vampire, a talking time-door, and several intelligent gas clouds.

" *It is not life as we know or understand it.* **"**

Things may not be quite so wild in your line of work, but have you ever tried talking to the guy who swaps over the rented office plants for near-identical copies every three months? He too has his story.

Vulcans approach everything with an open mind. They live in pursuit of knowledge, **not in pursuit of proving that they know it all already**, as many humans do.

An open mind is a delightful thing, but it is not always the sign of a warm, open nature. Mr. Spock would never greet Dr. McCoy by asking him if he was having a good day. To the truly open-minded, that information is irrelevant. Equally, telling someone to "have a nice day" would never occur to Spock in a million years. And especially, perhaps, when speaking to Dr. McCoy. After all, what a desolate vacuum of interesting experience a *"nice day"* can be. Spock would never wish that on you.

We generally like to think of ourselves as open-minded if we are free from the prejudices of our day, and if we occasionally join our partner in listening to the Klingon opera channel. But there is a much bigger outcome to this Spock-like thinking than many realize. A truly open mind can be set free from the habit of worry.

There is a Vulcan folk tale, dating back to their warrior past, of an old *plomeek* farmer whose son is injured falling off his pet *sehlat* **(a sort of fanged bear)**. Everyone expresses their sympathy, but the farmer says, *"Who is to define if it is a good or a bad thing?"*

The next day, the local warlord's army arrives, drafting young men into battle – all except the old farmer's son, who is injured. His neighbors are envious, resentful

even, of his luck. But the farmer knows better. **"Who is to define if it is a good or a bad thing?"** he muses.

The army goes on to win an easy battle, and the neighbors' sons come home hailed as heroes, and showered with rewards (as this is Vulcan they were probably book tokens). But the farmer ponders to himself, **"Who is to define if it is a good or a bad thing?"**

After all, the next battle may not be so successful, and the soldiers might be coming home with a nasty case of neck pinch.

And so it goes. The outcome is never conclusive until the day you die. And in Mr. Spock's case, not necessarily even then.

Having an open mind gives you an edge in problem-solving. On his original five-year mission, Spock encounters some miners who are being terrorized by a flesh-melting monster. The miners' response is to try and kill it. They are also baffled by the existence of strange spheres of silicon in the mines.

Spock's open mind puts these two puzzles together and comes up with a wonderful answer. Spock is prepared to consider life *"but not as we know or understand it."* He works out that the spheres are in fact the eggs of the creature that is attacking them. The monstrous killer is a mother. Spock manages to keep the eggs safe and even sets up a lucrative business relationship in which the baby monsters dig tunnels for the miners – possibly putting a whole tunnel-digging crew out of work, but that's another story.

Of course, being open-minded doesn't mean you should never wish anyone a nice day. But being mindful, our day ahead – **WHETHER IT'S NICE OR NOT** – can still involve something as amazing as a talking gas cloud or a friendly rock monster.

" *You insist on applying human standards...*

Vulcans are flexible in their thinking. They don't expect aliens to think like them or act like them and they are quick to see a new point of view. When Captain Kirk discovers an alien society in which innocent primitives worship a computer, he wants to overthrow it. Spock, however, is happy to leave well alone. If another planet isn't broken, he reasons, don't fix it. Humans tend to think their values should rule the universe. Not so Spock, who

...to non-human cultures. **"**

tells Kirk, **"I remind you that humans are only a tiny minority in this galaxy."**

Spock would point out that even on Earth, we are just a minority – compared to creatures like ants, krill, and bristlemouth fish.

SO IS IT LOGICAL FOR US TO TREAT EVEN THIS WORLD AS IF IT IS OURS?

3

ON LIVING IN
THE MOMENT

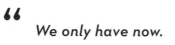

We only have now.

Vulcans know that by living in the **NOW** they are able to make clearer judgments. They are not distracted by the mistakes of the past or anxieties about what could be. They act without self-consciousness or fear of embarrassment. Instead, they concentrate on the experience of the present, paying complete attention to it.

There are many benefits to the Vulcan art of living in the **NOW**, including some *unexpected pleasures*. For instance, have you ever wondered why ice creams tasted better when we were children? Because we lived completely in the moment when we ate them. We enjoyed every lick as if it was the last. Today, it is almost impossible to order an ice cream or piece of cake without a family member or friend cheerfully pointing out that it is going to kill us. The baggage of knowledge intrudes on the **NOW**.

Mr. Spock would enjoy an ice cream in the same way as our childhood selves, because he, like all Vulcans, lives in the moment. Except he would be more likely to order *plomeek* soup if he wanted a treat, something purple and Vulcan and filled with, er... *plomeek*.

While traveling back to our time — to save the world, naturally — Spock and Kirk visit a sea life park to inspect a pair of whales they are going to need. Desiring to know if the whales would be okay to travel on short notice (whales do have pretty full diaries), Kirk seeks an expert to consult. Spock simply jumps right into the pool and asks the whales. Well, he does have the advantage of the Vulcan mind-meld. It is an act of totally in-the-now practicality that someone racked by self-consciousness would never do.

BUT IT IS VERY SPOCK.

The Vulcan philosopher Surak teaches us the past is only useful if we can learn from it. Experience can be a dangerous guide as it would be illogical to assume that any two situations are exactly the same. Thinking about the future is only relevant if, through our own actions, we can alter the probable outcomes. The future begins in the present. Do not think about what could be. Think about what is. Then act in a way that leads logically to the desired outcome.

Living in the now is an important part of mindfulness. Ancient Tao wisdom from the planet Earth tells us that we should avoid thoughts of the future. They make us fearful or greedy. Much of what we fear never comes to pass. The Vulcan philosopher Sorvin once remarked, *"I am an old man and have known many troubles, but most of them never happened."*

Similarly, reflecting on past failures does not bring wisdom so much as negativity. The Ferengi politician Quig said, *"I have learned from my mistakes and believe I can repeat them exactly."* That is the danger living in the past brings with it.

In Shakespeare's play **Hamlet**, the Prince is tired of living with endless speculation. He concludes that in the end it is worthless. He finally decides, *"the readiness is all."* Of course, it sounds better in the original Klingon. Mr. Spock would relate to this. And he would probably make a better Hamlet, too. Spock would make a swift job of bringing down his father's killer, by delivering fewer speeches and setting his phaser to stun.

In Spock's early career on the *U.S.S. DISCOVERY*, it seems humankind is doomed by an artificial intelligence that has some knowledge of the future. Others fear that this knowledge gives the enemy an unbeatable advantage. Spock thinks otherwise, his pragmatic Vulcan view giving him a total belief in the power of acting in the present: *"Now does matter. What happened before no longer exists, what will happen next has not yet been written. We have only now."*

This sees Spock agreeing with another brilliant mind. Human genius Albert Einstein said, *"Past is dead, future is uncertain; present is all you have, so eat drink and live merry."*

Spock does not go quite that far, since living merry would not be a priority to a Vulcan. With all sentient life in the Galaxy in peril, a chorus of "If you're happy and you know it" might not be appropriate. Instead, he makes use of his favorite game, 3-D Chess, for a very motivating metaphor. *"The board,"* he points out to his adopted sister, Michael, *"is yours."*

We must be mindful of the moves we make. Whether it's diving into a whale tank or choosing to eat a particularly dangerous ice cream, the one thing it would be illogical to do with the power of **NOW** is waste it. Your chance to change the future is here, right now. And you don't have an all-powerful artificial intelligence about to attack you.

THE BOARD IS YOURS...

" Nothing unreal exists. "

Given his encounters with space gods, bodiless beings, and sentient computers, Spock's life may appear pretty fantastical. But in fact, Vulcans are deeply practical. Their lack of room for fuzzy thinking is encapsulated by Kir-Kin-Tha's first law of metaphysics: "Nothing unreal exists."

This simple insight has its advantages. When the crew are placed in a perfect illusion of a Wild West setting, Spock deduces it is unreal when one of McCoy's tranquilizers doesn't work. His reasoning is thus: "Physical reality is consistent with universal laws. Where the laws do not operate, there is no reality. All of this is unreal." He is even prepared to take a bullet to prove it. When enemies fire at Spock, he simply refuses to believe in them. NATURALLY, FOR SPOCK IT WORKS.

Maybe some things that appear to threaten you will disappear if you cease to believe in them. Some matters of the mind, paranoia and superstition can be conquered.

Vulcans are not easily prey to tricks and illusion. When a powerful alien called Sylvia attempts to scare an *Enterprise* landing party, she unleashes dark visions, cackling witches, and evil spells.

> "Winds shall rise and fogs descend,
> So leave here all or meet your end."

When asked to comment by Kirk, Spock merely replies, "Very bad poetry, Captain."

4

ON LOVE

Many things are easier in the 23rd century, but romance — well, not so much. Especially if you work in space. If you meet the perfect partner, they may well be an android, an alien shape-shifter, or possibly an illusion drawn from your own mind. Ask Captain Kirk — he has dated all three. Mr. Spock, however, has rarely been a victim of Cupid's arrow. **VULCANS ARE EVEN LOGICAL ABOUT LOVE**.

On the planet Vulcan, partners are chosen for rational reasons. There is no swiping left or right on a dating app, and no having one too many Romulan ales and shouting, *"I love you!"* at someone across a crowded holosuite. Vulcan families decide the weddings of their children on a sensible analysis of character and mutual interests. Frankly, they probably look at your 3-D chess results, too. And if the happy couple don't like the arrangement, it's all easily sorted out with a traditional duel to the death.

SIMPLE.

As adults, Vulcans have a powerful urge to mate, known as *Pon Farr*, which comes round every seven years. Many of us humans do with a lot less frequent action, another reason to be jealous of them.

Spock himself has taken part in the ceremony of *Pon Farr*. He went to Vulcan to be joined with his betrothed, T'Pring, but she had other plans. Sadly, in the 23rd century, dumping someone by text is not acceptable. To get herself out of the arranged marriage T'Pring had to force Spock to take part in a ritual death duel. *Infinitely more civilized.* Spock won the duel but then freed his betrothed from her vows.

He had no regret about losing T-Pring. He told his rival Stonn, *"After a time you may find that having is not so pleasing a thing after all as wanting. It may not be logical but it is often true."*

Ouch! A nice little zinger to leave the happy couple with. Here, there is a hint of agreement with the noted Ferengi wit, Grand Nagus Vock, who declared, *"One should always be in love. That is the reason one should never marry."*

Spock may appear uninterested in romance but he is no fool when it comes to understanding what it means to others. He has no illusions about how badly a failed relationship can turn out. On one occasion, the *Starship Enterprise* crossed the Neutral Zone to encounter the Romulans. A Romulan commander believed that Spock

was in love with her. However, his dalliance turned out to be part of a sneaky scam to steal an important military secret, the Romulan cloaking device. Spock was exposed as a deceiver.

Did he try to appeal to the Romulan's soft heart? Did he attempt to trade on their recent sweet nothings?

" *...having is not so pleasing a thing after all as wanting. It may not be logical but it is often true.* **"**

Nope, he simply asked her, *"What is your present form of execution?"*

You might try that line next time you deeply offend a potential life-partner.

Spock did have one carefree, happy relationship. On the paradise planet of Omicron Ceti III, he fell in love with an old flame. Had he finally found his true love? In fact, he had been zapped in the face by some weird alien flowers. Let's not forget his cosmic lifestyle brings unique complications.

Spock did say that this romance was the only time he had been **truly happy.** He was, however, quick to give it up when he realized the fuzzy feeling was an illusion. This is truly mindful, since Spock is preferring truth to a conventional idea of happiness. Mindfulness like this,

LOOKING REALITY IN THE FACE, is not always a shortcut to bliss.

We humans are unlikely to adopt Vulcan traditions, but we can learn from a mindful approach to love. We can start by listening carefully to our partner, instead of drifting off and wondering what time *THE WRATH OF KHAN* is on the Revenge Channel tonight.

A mindful person will accept their partner as they are, instead of as they want them to be. If they are an android, built by a solitary mad scientist, at least it cuts down on half the wedding invitations. If they are an alien shape-shifter, then there is probably a special edition of the cosmic *Kama Sutra* you can Google. The possibilities are literally endless.

Vulcans have created strong traditions around marriage, as love rather confounds their ideas of rational thought. We can admire their ideas without perhaps ever agreeing with four tuneful Vulcan minstrels who famously sang, **"ALL YOU NEED IS LOGIC."**

5

ON FAMILY

" *I have some business to conduct with schoolmates... A demonstration of the Vulcan neck pinch.* **"**

The 23rd century contains many things we find hard to believe, but one of the weirdest is that everyone learns to get along. In the workplace (and by "in the workplace," I mean on the *Starship Enterprise*), there is little friction between races, rich, poor, green, blue, artificial, and organic ... However, reassuringly, some tension does still exist in this apparent social paradise – **AND ITS NAME IS... FAMILY.**

Even calm, rational Vulcans have family rifts, father-son issues, awkward silences... in fact, they can have awkward silences that last a couple of decades. Yes, there was a time when Spock and his dad did not communicate for 18 Earth years. That's even more years in Vulcan time, which some sources work out as 266.4 Earth days per year. Do the math yourself **(IF YOU'RE VULCAN)**.

A great rift occurred because Spock's dad wanted him to go to the Vulcan Science Academy, and wild, crazy young Spock became a Starfleet officer instead. *How miffed would Sarek have been if Spock had run away with the circus? Or had become a tribble-grooming specialist?*

Vulcan parent-child relations are complicated. Having given their child a good education, fed them healthy *plomeek* soup, and taught them the Vulcan nerve pinch, there seems little for the aloof, practical father to talk to his offspring about. This is not planet Earth where fathers and sons can spend countless hours arguing over how to barbecue a Klingon *targ*-burger or who left that dent on the shuttlecraft.

Just because Sarek has nothing to say to Spock, this does not reflect any disrespect. In fact, he berates his wife for embarrassing his son in front of his colleagues. Effectively, he seeks to protect Spock, but without his son knowing. Being seen to care would probably give Sarek a heart attack – **WHEREVER THAT PARTICULAR ORGAN IS**.

Spock, likewise, bears no resentment for his father's cold shoulder. He has a clear picture of Sarek's merits

and abilities, unclouded by sentiment. In fact, when a murderer is loose on the ship, Spock helpfully points out that his father has precisely the skill necessary to kill a man. With equal logic, he later risks his own life to donate blood to save his father, as he is the only one who can do so.

Good old Sarek, of course, does not thank Spock for saving his life, as his son pursued the only logical course of action. And, **"One does not thank logic."**

We humans find it harder to make rational choices, and to see clearly when loved ones are involved. We sign our bookworm kid up for the boxing team, tell our deepest secrets to the gossipy sister, and enter our ugliest pets for beauty contests. Logic seems to go out of the window where our nearest and dearest are concerned. But **some mindful clarity of thought can help our relationships**. Is Dad really happy we bought him a subscription to *Slowing Down* magazine, or would he perhaps have preferred a Ferengi energy whip?

Luckily for Spock, he has a human mother who is ready to shower him with affection. Except, emotionally, Spock has his umbrella up. Amanda is disappointed that after many years among humans, Spock has not learned to smile. This may be a simple observation on his formal demeanor, or possibly she paid for an expensive Vulcan

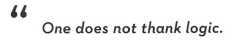

One does not thank logic.

Science Academy home tutorial program on raising both corners of the mouth simultaneously. We will never know.

Humans grow up with the naïve but wonderful belief that their parents know everything. *Vulcans grow up with the same belief... but, in their case, their parents really do know everything.* Well, everything except how to smile at their children. We humans sometimes experience disappointment on discovering our dads are merely human. Spock, of course, will never have that problem.

Although Vulcans don't make their feelings obvious, they are deeply connected to their offspring. Tuvok, the Vulcan security officer on *Starship Voyager*, is forced to be separate from his children, but he says they are part of him and he is incomplete without them. He is clearly proud of his children, who have mastered several states of heightened awareness at an age when Earth kids still have stabilizers on their jet packs.

Being mindful about family relationships does not mean being as frank as a Vulcan about your parents. In families a little honesty can often do a lot of harm. But you could get your children to go to sleep by threatening to sing them a Vulcan lullaby about enlightenment... there is always something to learn from **OUR GREEN-BLOODED FRIENDS.**

ON SELF-
ACCEPTANCE

5

Vulcans have a certain edge over humans. They are three times as strong as us. They live longer. They have better eyebrow-raising skills. **AND THEY ARE ALSO INSULT-PROOF.**

The 23rd century is a more enlightened time than ours, but strangely the cheap insult is far from extinct. Phrases like *"pointy-eared, green-blooded hobgoblin"* are far from rare (we're looking at you, Dr. McCoy) but Mr. Spock could not care less. **IT'S A SELF-ACCEPTANCE THING.**

Vulcans do not do self-delusion. When told by Captain Kirk he is "mutinous and computerized," Spock replies, *"...computerized is inaccurate. A machine can be computerized, not a man."* When routinely labeled by Dr. McCoy as inhuman and cold-blooded, Spock simply finds it a satisfactory description of himself. And, as the Vulcan philosopher Smorik once observed,

"Marauding alien clones may break my bones,
But names will never hurt me."

When the godlike being Apollo says he does not want Spock on his world as he wants no sad faces, Kirk asks if Spock is offended. Spock's reaction is, *"Insults are only effective when emotion is present."*

This is a mindful observation. We bring emotion to insults when they hit us personally. The awkward fact is, insults hurt when they contain some truth. After all, no one could offend you by calling you "dinosaur-face," since it is unlikely you have a face like a dinosaur. The insult simply has no power — unless you are a Gorn, of course, then you **DO** look like a dinosaur.

But if someone insults your looks, or your taste in Borg cosmetic implants — and it hurts, then it follows that maybe you have some insecurity in that department.

This is not a problem for Vulcans.

If their mothers do indeed wear army boots, they will happily acknowledge it. In fact, Vulcans are mostly puzzled by insults. If they are true, then they are merely observations. If they are untrue, then they are pointless.

"
*Be mindful, but set your
phaser to stun.*
"

Of course, it does not help to become someone's scratching post. Even Spock will send a subtle jibe back occasionally. When told by Kirk he is getting more human all the time, he replies, *"I see no reason to stand here and be insulted."*

The worst thing you can say to a Vulcan is that they are illogical and emotional. This is effectively saying that they are not very good at being Vulcan. And all Vulcans know that it really is much better to be Vulcan than anything else.

Being half-Vulcan, half-human, Spock has always had to take criticism both ways. On the *Enterprise*, he's called a machine, and back home, as a child, he was sniped at for being an emotional "Earther." No wonder he took refuge in the friendship of his pet *sehlat* (that grizzly-sized beast with six-inch fangs). Experience taught Spock the value of both cultures. On one occasion when he traveled back in time, he even managed to give some comfort to his younger self:

"There is some human blood in my family line. It is not fatal."

In contrast to Spock, we humans do do self-delusion. We think Aluura from Accounts will be upset if we don't sign her birthday card. We think the holodeck simulation of Stephen Hawking really loves our theories, and we think the boss will miss our input if we arrive 10 minutes late for work.

In the Vulcan fable, "The Lara Bird and the Giant Sandworm," a little lara bird lands on the back of a 25-foot sandworm. After a while, it asks permission to leave. The monster worm says, *"I didn't notice you arrive, so I won't notice if you leave."*

For the giant sandworm, read your boss.

It is not easy to break through those comforting layers of illusion we have built up to make life that little bit easier. We have one law for ourselves, another for the rest. It goes something like this...

I'M AN EXPERT – YOU ARE A BLOWHARD. I'M RESOURCEFUL – YOU ARE SNEAKY. I'M CUDDLY – YOU ARE FAT.

The Andorian diplomat, Tarel, is supposed to have found the head of the Imperial Guard, Shrokor, so objectionable that she told him, *"If you were my husband, I'd poison your ale."* Shrokor apparently replied, *"If you were my wife, I'd drink it."* Shrokor didn't bother to deny that he was objectionable. In fact, he prided himself on it. And in a public row, any defensive remark would make him appear weak. The smart way out was self-acceptance.

Facing ourselves as we really are is the first step to not having to be that way. If you finally accept that you are a bad listener, it means, miraculously, you have started listening. And listening is a mindful activity, whether your ears are pointy or not.

" *Infinite Diversity...*

Vulcans may appear conservative and stuffy on first acquaintance, but they are in fact very open-minded compared to many races – including our own. The Vulcan belief is summed up by the term IDIC – Infinite Diversity in Infinite Combinations. In simple terms, Vulcans refer to **"the combination of a number of things to make existence worthwhile."**

...*in Infinite Combinations.* 🎵🎵

That's why a Vulcan will make friends with a sentient rock, shoot the breeze with a glowing cloud, enjoy small talk with a microbe, and share a song with a whale. And the Vulcan will happily take the side of any of these things in an argument against humanity.

But be warned (if you are a Klingon) that love of diversity does not include wedgie-givers, moustache-twirlers, queue-jumpers, and sunbed-hoggers. Vulcans are open-minded, but not open to being walked over.

Even Spock took a conventional view of a punk on a bus in one of his time-travel adventures to Earth. When he asked for the music to be turned down, and the punk turned it up louder, Spock applied the Vulcan nerve pinch to silence his music. Infinite diversity is a wonderful thing, but you are still allowed to know what you like.

7
ON TRUTH

" *The Truth does not seek*
to make friends. **"**

Vulcans are known for their truthfulness. We humans surround ourselves with a web of lies just to get through the day. Mr. Spock does not. He frequently tells his captain that he is wrong, and would definitely tell a good friend that he was deluded about that waitress on Starbase II. He would also respond honestly when asked whether someone's bum looked big in that dress. Even if that someone was a big green alien monster.

As the philosopher Surak once said, *"The Truth does not seek to make friends."* Everyday honesty is routine for Vulcans, who prefer to deal with unvarnished facts. If a Vulcan was told that they smelled bad, they would accept this as a fact and shower without question or emotion. If a human was told the same thing, they might well burst into tears. A Klingon, of course, would feel quietly pleased.

Being honest is harder for us weaker-minded humans. We are all told as children to tell the truth. Then we're told off for saying we want the biggest slice of cake on the plate. We are asked if we would like to do some helpful chores for Mommy, then bawled out for our honest reply, which is, of course, "No."

Naturally we grow into confused adults. Not so Vulcans, who cut cakes with maddening precision — so there isn't a biggest bit — and do not require *liking* jobs to be an important part of doing them.

For humans, the rewards of telling the truth appear highly debatable. **Forgiveness doesn't always follow a truthful admission.** Try telling your friends the holiday place you booked has no wifi, and not even the most basic force field.

Let's look at some everyday situations where the truth is not an asset. A friend asks us what we really think of their love poetry. Or they ask for a frank opinion on their nose-ring. A colleague asks if we'd like to try the dish of live serpent worms they brought in...

Other questions that the truth is rarely able to handle include: How much do you drink in the average week?

Your doctor generally doubles your answer. Or perhaps: *"Was your ex better than me?"*

Despite their devotion to the truth, even a Vulcan would advise against answering this last question entirely honestly. Vulcans are many things but not naïve. Surak also said, *"It is not a lie to keep the truth to oneself."*

Nevertheless, few Vulcans like to admit that they lie. When Saavik discovers that Spock and Kirk have misled their enemy Khan, she challenges Spock saying, *"You lied?"* He responds, *"I exaggerated."*

And he would surely advise you to do the same when confronted by a genetically engineered, homicidal maniac.

Spock's search for truth is a part of his own journey. He looks for philosophical truth, not mere, mechanical honesty. In short, Vulcans are logical people, who prefer truth but are not slaves to it. Thus, Mr. Spock will lie... **IF IT IS LOGICAL TO DO SO**.

" *It is not a lie to keep the truth to oneself.* "

"Vulcans never bluff."

Much of the Galaxy believes that Vulcans are incapable of lying, or even bluffing, but this may just be because Vulcans don't play poker so they haven't been found out. Vulcans exaggerate, conceal their identities, and omit certain

Except ...

inconvenient facts, but they find it very convenient for the rest of the universe to believe that they are completely truthful at all times.

Vulcans go to a lot of trouble to convince people not to mess with them. When the Vulcans first made contact with the Klingons, a Vulcan ship was lost. The Vulcans realized they were dealing with a race that was ready to rumble and created a policy that became known as the **"Vulcan Hello."**

No, this was not a mindful way of greeting the Klingons courteously. This was not **"A zillion blessings on your beautifully contoured head"**...

...IT WAS A PULVERIZING WEAPONS' BARRAGE

The Vulcans knew that the warlike Klingons would only respect open hostility. In fact, as connoisseurs of strength and

battle, they loved it! Anything less than the death of many of their finest warriors they would have taken as an insult. The calculated annihilation of their kind paved the way for eventual peace and understanding between the two races.

It was a good thing the Klingons thought the peace-loving Vulcans couldn't possibly be bluffing or there would have been a massive and bloody war.

Vulcans are very careful about when they are caught lying, so they don't fib often. When they do, it's for important reasons, like not telling the Klingons you are an undercover Starfleet officer or that you only have a pair of twos.

IF YOU'RE GOING TO BLUFF, MAKE SURE NO ONE THINKS YOU ARE...

8

ON FEELINGS

Vulcans do not like to show their feelings. On their planet, sales of pink heart cushions, with *"I love you"* embroidered on them, are on the low side. Birthday cards say things like, *"It is logical to assume your age has increased once more. Get over it."* On the downside, you miss simple joys like the shared elation of celebrating the last-minute victory of your local Sudoku team. *But on the upside you don't have to hug Aunt T'Prong* on Pagan Festival Day.

Feelings are especially tricky for Spock. As he is half-human, there is no "road map" as to how to behave. After coming back from the dead (another "no road-map" situation), Spock's mental state is tested by a computer. He sails through the mind-boggling math and logic conundrums with ease. The only question that throws him is: **HOW DO YOU FEEL?**

The answer to that one is not in a text book. Feelings are a topic that Spock frequently discusses with Dr. McCoy. *"The release of emotion is what keeps us*

"
The release of emotion is
what keeps us healthy.
Dr. McCoy
"

healthy. Emotionally healthy." McCoy tells him.
"That may be, Doctor," Spock replies. *"However, I
have noted that the healthy release of emotion is
frequently unhealthy for those closest to you."*

On Vulcan, feelings are present, but showing them is
considered bad taste.

There was a time when Spock thought that the removal of all emotion might be the way ahead. Possibly this could pave the way for a job in 24th-century life insurance. *"I'm sorry Ma'am, but assimilation by the Borg is not covered in your claim. Technically your hubby has not died. In fact, he may now live forever. No pay out."* You can see it might be an advantage.

In seeking to be drained of all emotion, Spock mind-melded with a vast living machine called *V'Ger*. It was not a magical moment for him. He found *V'Ger* barren.

"No mystery, no hope," he reflected. And finally he concluded, *"No answers."* You see, even in the book of life, Spock's Vulcan side was expecting the answers to be at the back.

It is an opinion frequently expressed by Captain Kirk that it is our emotions that make us human, giving us an edge on computers. Yet it is our feelings that make life most uncomfortable for us.

Wouldn't it be nice to be able to visit those annoying

relatives with our feelings switched off? We could face the boasting about their holographic masseur more calmly. Or the endless humble brags about their kids. *"The twins just made the Starfleet officer program, but then they aren't nine yet."*

Remember Shakespeare: *"A coward dies a thousand times before his death, but the valiant taste of death but once."* This can be applied to the lesser dramas of life. *"A coward anticipates his mother's plomeek soup a thousand times, the valiant taste of it but once."*

In Vulcan philosophy, the parable of the Second *Lirpa* is used to warn us of the damage done to ourselves through our emotions. It goes like this: imagine you are walking along and some maniac whacks you on the head with the blunt end of their traditional weapon, the *lirpa*. You are in great pain. Now, would you respond to this event by asking the same loony if you can borrow his weapon... **AND THEN WHACKING YOURSELF IN THE SAME PLACE?**

Frankly, it wouldn't help. But when we suffer a setback in life — a missed promotion, an attack by evolved nanites, a transformation into an octahedral cube of basic minerals — we often react in a similar way, by viewing our plight from all the worst angles, tormenting ourselves by contemplating the worst possible outcomes — piling on the emotional agony.

Surak tells us the first setback is unavoidable. But the second blow of the lirpa **is a matter of our own choice.**

Here's an everyday example. You are out shopping and see a cool pair of rocket boots. You are going to buy them when your partner shakes their head. Uh-uh! The boots are a no-no. They refuse to explain. You are at first puzzled, then hurt. Do they think your days of extreme sports are over? Will you have to throw out your time-travel suit too?

Wounded, you wander the Earth, a shadow of your old self. Then your birthday comes, you open your gifts and discover that your partner had already bought you the same rocket boots. That was why they didn't want you to purchase them. Suddenly you realize you wasted two weeks of self-doubt. **YOUR SECOND *LIRPA* WAS TIPPED WITH FALSE DATA.** And as someone once said, "Insufficient facts always invite danger." Yes, that was Spock too.

Of course, no question baffles Spock for too long, even "How do you feel?" When saying goodbye to his father, he asks him to relay a message to his mother. It may be short, but to her it will mean a great deal, an admission that her human world of feeling is real to Spock too. "Tell her I feel fine."

And, taken with some mindful perspective, Spock is saying: **IT'S FINE TO FEEL.**

> ## " *The needs of the many outweigh the needs of the few...*

One of Spock's most famous quotes comes when he risks his own life to save the crew of the *Enterprise* from the Genesis Effect – a kind of mini-Big Bang. Spock saves his ship but in the course of doing so, he microwaves himself beyond repair. On his sacrifice, Spock observes, "The needs of the many outweigh the needs of the few... or the one."

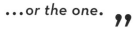

...or the one. **,,**

The logic would appear to be rock solid. But it is also devastating. It means the end of Spock. Is there a flaw in this memorable saying?

THERE MAY BE ANOTHER "EXCEPT" COMING...

Except...

There is a certain irony in the phrase "the needs of the many..." being so well known, because Spock grew to question it later. When Captain Kirk risked everything to bring Spock back to life, Kirk inverted his logic, saying, **"The needs of the one outweigh the needs of the many."**

Kirk believed that one soul could not be measured by mere math. Effectively, he was saying that Spock's life, his example, is important enough to take risks for. Who is going to disagree? Certainly not Spock, who could find no snappy comeback at the time. (Kirk did once say that his first officer's modesty did not stand close examination).

Then, on their next mission, Spock was prepared to risk the ship to save one man: Chekov. Was it the logical thing to do? Spock was forced to admit, "It was the human thing to do." This is part of his journey. During Kirk's first five-year mission, Spock often denied his humanity, delighted in his differences as a Vulcan, and felt insulted

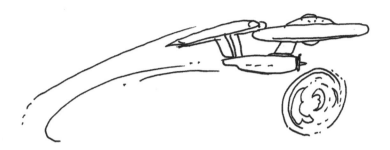

when accused of human behavior. But, he is mindful – open to change. The fun he had saving the universe with his *Enterprise* pals, and the lessons he learned from dealing with crazy risk-takers like Captain Kirk and passionate, "kill-them-or-cure-them" types like McCoy, led him to accept his humanity. Basically, the illogical people seemed not to be completely stupid...

Look at yourself. Are you an Original Series Spock, or an evolved, Movie Spock? Do you deny the flawed side of your nature or have you come to terms with it, even learned to enjoy it?

WOULD YOU SAVE CHEKOV OR LEAVE HIM BEHIND?

9

ON CHANGE

Are you sitting in a damp cave, rubbing two sticks together, while eating cold mammoth blubber for breakfast? Probably not, and yet you are probably one of those countless humans who complain about that awful thing: change. It hasn't worked out too badly for us, has it? And yet we grumble about every little change in our lives, the new transporter noise, the healthier replicator menus, or the update to the holodeck – I mean, why can't you get that Orion detective program any more?

Change can be tough for us humans, but not so for the open-minded Vulcan. In their dark ages, the Vulcans almost wiped themselves out in a series of terrible wars. The desire for survival forced them to change from proud, emotional beings to calm, rational ones. It turned them into a gentle, peace-loving people – who can hurl you across a room.

Vulcan philosophy is all about accepting change. In fact, Mr. Spock has stated: ***"Change is the essential process of all existence."***

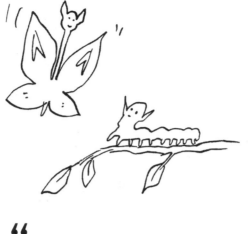

"

Change is the essential
process of all existence.

"

The Vulcan philosopher Sorvin commented, **"Without one second changing into another, how could we experience life?** And yet there are those who regret time passing by. What system would they prefer? One where time stood still? Nothing would ever happen. That was tried on a universal scale before the event humans call the Big Bang. It wasn't that interesting and so it was... **CHANGED.**"

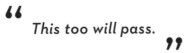

This too will pass.

And by the way, **"Big Bang"** is an illogical name. You can't hear a bang in space. Vulcans call it the **"Silent Splurge"** — although that does sound classier in the original Vulcan.

Spock's observation on change is clearly true. If an egg never turned into a chicken, how could it cross the road? If larvae never turned into worms how could Klingons enjoy their lunch?

Lost in the mists of time are the origins of the tale about the impermanence of all things. It seems that once a great Vulcan ruler challenged his adviser to come up with a piece of wisdom that would always be true, that he could engrave on his favorite *lirpa*. After some thought, the wise man took away the weapon and engraved upon it the words, **"This too will pass."**

Not a crowd-pleaser on the face of it. I mean, it's no **"If you can read this you're too close."** Or **"My other car is warp capable,"** but **LOGICAL**, and also **LIBERATING**.

"This too will pass," is a chastening thought if you are feeling on top of the world, and a comforting thought if you are low. The warlord was impressed, and didn't use the lirpa to cut the wise man's head off (which is what happens in the Klingon version of this tale).

Certainly the wise Vulcan chose one of the few phrases that will always remain true. And if you doubt the wisdom in this story, don't worry... **THAT FEELING WILL PASS TOO**.

Galactic myth suggests that Vulcans are incapable of making mistakes. It was even claimed that they only put erasers on the ends of pencils as a courtesy to visiting humans. But the ability to learn from error and change is vital to growth. The Andorian Shrokor said, *"To improve is to change; to be perfect is to change often."* Spock would agree with this.

Vulcans are calm about change even when it seems to be against their interests. When the *Enterprise* crew entered the Mirror Universe, one where goodies were baddies, the alternate Mr. Spock calmly accepted that the evil Terran Empire would collapse. He could see his society's downfall and had no interest in preventing it. It was simply what must happen. The Mirror Spock remained wise, even though he came from a different culture and had a very **EVIL BEARD**.

This approach is reminiscent of the views of the ancient Chinese Tao wisdom, which sees the universe as sacred. The Way of the Tao regards the world as already perfect and says it should be accepted as it is. So learn to appreciate a changing universe — you may just be stuck with it. And Vulcans would also say, don't fear having to change yourself. To quote a Vulcan proverb, *"Only jumbo mollusks never change their minds."*

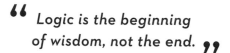
" Logic is the beginning of wisdom, not the end. "

It would be wonderful if there was a system for getting life right all the time, and it would be great if it could be sold in book form. Not yet, I'm afraid. Even in the 24th century, they live on the edge of disaster seemingly on a daily basis. If we were all perfectly adjusted human beings, then where would our great songs of heartbreak come from? Our funniest comedians, our least sensible romantic encounters? Can it be life's imperfections that make it sometimes seem... kind of perfect?

Logic is the cornerstone of Spock's thought as a younger man, but if you bought this book thinking it was the magic bullet that would solve all your problems, then think again. As he grew older, Spock learned that there are some things logic can't solve. Matters of love, matters of destiny – *or weird problems like how to stop a giant space machine gobbling up the Earth*.

Rational thought had been a good guide to Spock. But that was all it was – a guide. The traveler has to walk the road themselves. We often enjoy our holidays more by throwing away the guide book and spending a night on the dodgy paradise planet that was not recommended by the experts.

COSMIC QUOTATION COINCIDENCES

Readers with an interest in cosmic coincidence may be interested to see some examples of great minds thinking alike on different worlds.

ON KEEPING AN OPEN MIND

The Vulcan folk tale of **the boy who fell off the *sehlat*** is very similar to a folk tale from China, on planet Earth.

ON LIVING IN THE MOMENT

The Vulcan philosopher Sorvin's remarks on having known **many troubles** are similar to those of human author Mark Twain. The deeply pedantic Sorvin is notable for many things including trying to have the word "sundown" removed from the Vulcan dictionary, as there is no up and down in space and, even if there was, the sun doesn't actually "set" at all, but remains where it is while other heavenly bodies revolve around it. Sadly, he failed, but he didn't feel sad of course, because he was a Vulcan.

Ferengi politician Quig, on knowing how to **repeat his mistakes,** is sharing a sentiment once voiced by 20th-century Earth satirist, Peter Cook. In fact, Quig faced a Federation court for repeating many financial "mistakes" that had come out in his own favor, and was charged with not only premeditated fraud, but also **prememorized crimes.** He was considered a brilliant mind until, in a confused business deal, he accidentally sold his vital organs to the Klingons while he was still using them. As he had already spent their credits, they came to collect.

"The readiness is all." Bizarrely, when Earth introduced its culture across space, it was astonished to find that within a short time, many other cultures, notably the Klingons, were quick to claim Shakespeare as their own. Vulcan philosopher T'Lek calls this **The Sherlock Syndrome,** as most races seem to have their own Holmes. Spock, in fact, has claimed that he is descended from the Vulcan equivalent of Holmes, Investgator Vo'nar.

ON LOVE

The noted Ferengi wit, Grand Nagus Vock, shares the views of the great human writer, Oscar Wilde. Vock, a great business mind, is renowned for striking a deal with his future self, who on his death bed, bequeathed his wealth to himself before he had earned it. The matter is still under temporal investigative review.

The Vulcan song **"All you Need is Logic"** has been observed as having similarities with a song by the 20th-century Earth group, The Beatles. Similarities between great minds, the Vulcan minstrels have pointed out, is *"only logical."*

ON SELF-ACCEPTANCE

The Vulcan fable of **The Lara Bird and the Giant Sandworm** has echoes of Aesop's fable of the mosquito and the bull. The exchange between Andorian diplomat Tarel and Imperial Guard leader Shrokor is intriguing in its similarity to one between 20th-century human politician Nancy Astor and her leader Winston Churchill. Not such

a great leader, Shrokor once led an Andorian fleet into an unstable wormhole. If you have seen him anywhere, will you let us know?

ON FEELINGS

The Vulcan tale of **the Second Lirpa** has a close relative in the Buddhist parable of the Second Arrow.

ON CHANGE

The ancient Vulcan tale **"This too will pass"** echoes a tale from Ancient Persia on Earth.

"To improve is to change; to be perfect is to change often."
Once again, the Andorian Shrokor proves his affinity with Winston Churchill. Shrokor, in fact, did change his mind often, but paradoxically did not end up perfect – as his detractor Tarel was keen to point out.

SOURCES

All quotes are from Mr. Spock and the original *STAR TREK* series unless otherwise stated.

"Humans smile with so little provocation."
p2, 'Journey to Babel,' S2, E10

"Live long and prosper."
p7, 'Amok Time,' S2, E1

"Curious how often you humans manage to obtain that which you do not want." p13, 'Errand of Mercy,' S1, E26

"I've never stopped to look at clouds before, or rainbows…" p17, 'This Side of Paradise,' S1, E24

"Computers make excellent and efficient servants, but I have no wish to serve under them." p18, 'The Ultimate Computer,' S2, E24

"It is not life as we know or understand it." p23, 'Operation Annihilate,' S1, E29

"You insist on applying human standards to non-human cultures." pp28–29, 'The Apple,' S2, E5

"Now does matter. What happened before no longer exists, what will happen next has not yet been written. We have only now."
p36, *STAR TREK DISCOVERY*, 'Perpetual Infinity,' S2, E11

"Nothing unreal exists."
p38, *STAR TREK IV: THE VOYAGE HOME*

"After a time you may find that having is not so pleasing a thing after all as wanting. It may not be logical but it is often true."
p44, 'Amok Time,' S2, E1

"What is your present form of execution?"
p46, 'The Enterprise Incident,' S3, E2

"My father is quite capable of killing. Logically and efficiently." p53, ' Journey to Babel,' S2, E10

"One does not thank logic, Amanda."
p54, Sarek, 'Journey to Babel,' S2, E10

"Without followers, evil cannot spread."
'And The Children Shall Lead,' S3, E4

"Loss of life is to be mourned only if that life is wasted."
STAR TREK: THE ANIMATED SERIES, 'Yesteryear,' S1, E2

"Emotions are alien to me – I am a scientist."
'This Side of Paradise,' S1, E24

"Insults are only effective when emotion is present."
p61, 'Who Mourns For Adonais?' S2, E2

"There is some human blood in my family line. It is not fatal."
p64, *STAR TREK:* THE ANIMATED SERIES, 'Yesteryear,' S1, E2

"The combination of a number of things to make existence worthwhile." p66, 'The Savage Curtain,' S3, E22

"...Vulcans cannot lie."
Romulan Commander, 'The Enterprise Incident,' S3, E2

"It is not a lie to keep the truth to oneself."
p73, 'The Enterprise Incident,' S3, E2

"I exaggerated." p74, *STAR TREK II: THE WRATH OF KHAN*

"Vulcans never bluff." p76, 'The Doomsday Machine,' S2, E6

"However, I have noted that the healthy release of emotion is frequently unhealthy for those closest to you." p83, 'Plato's Stepchildren,' S3, E10

"Insufficient facts always invite danger." p87, 'Space Seed,' S1, E22

"The needs of the many outweigh the needs of the few." p88, *STAR TREK II: THE WRATH OF KHAN*

"The needs of the one... outweigh the needs of the many." p90, Captain Kirk, *STAR TREK III: THE SEARCH FOR SPOCK*

"Change is the essential process of all existence." p94, 'Let That Be Your Last Battlefield,' S3, E15

"Logic is the beginning of wisdom, not the end." p100, *STAR TREK VI: THE UNDISCOVERED COUNTRY*

In Memory of

Leonard Nimoy (1931–2015)
the original Vulcan

and

Dorothy 'D.C.' Fontana
(1939–2019)
the real matriarch of Vulcan
philosophy

"A life is like a garden. Perfect moments can be had, but not preserved, except in memory. LLAP"

Leonard Nimoy's Final Tweet